A FOOT IN
TWO
WORLDS

John Chapman

Guidebooks for Life 👥

Bible-based essentials
for your Christian journey

A Foot in Two Worlds is part of a series of
straightforward, practical Christian books from
Matthias Media which deal with the important
nuts-and-bolts topics that Christians need to know
about as we walk each day with our Master.

Some Christian books are all theory and no
practical application; others are all stories and
tips with no substance. The Guidebooks for Life
aim to achieve a vital balance—that is, to dig
into the Bible and discover what God is telling
us there, as well as applying that truth to our daily
Christian lives.

For up-to-date information about the latest
Guidebooks for Life, visit our website:
www.matthiasmedia.com.au

GUIDEBOOKS FOR LIFE

A FOOT IN
TWO
WORLDS

THE JOY AND STRUGGLE OF
THE NORMAL CHRISTIAN LIFE

John Chapman

matthiasmedia

A Foot in Two Worlds
© Matthias Media 2009

Matthias Media
(St Matthias Press Ltd ACN 067 558 365)
PO Box 225
Kingsford NSW 2032
Australia
Telephone: (02) 9663 1478; international: +61-2-9663-1478
Facsimile: (02) 9663 3265; international: +61-2-9663-3265
Email: info@matthiasmedia.com.au
Internet: www.matthiasmedia.com.au

Matthias Media (USA)
Telephone: 724 964 8152; international: +1-724-964-8152
Facsimile: 724 964 8166; international: +1-724-964-8166
Email: sales@matthiasmedia.com
Internet: www.matthiasmedia.com

ISBN 978 1 921441 34 9

Cover design and typesetting by Lankshear Design Pty Ltd.

For Peter and Betty Chiswell—
friends of long standing, and fine Christian leaders.

CONTENTS

Chapter 1

CHRISTIANITY IS NOT FOR WIMPS

I HAVE BEEN A CHRISTIAN for 60 years. That's a long time to give something a try, and it puts me in a position to strongly recommend it.

Over that time, two particular aspects of Christian living have surprised me. One is that it turned out to be so good; the other is that it turned out to be so hard.

I remember speaking to a group of men at Robb College at the University of New England, and I was explaining that God would forgive us for all our sins because of the death of the Lord Jesus. A young man said, "Are you saying that God will forget about my past?"

"That is exactly what I am saying", I replied.

The tears welled up in his eyes and he said, "That's nearly too good to be true".

"It seems like it, but it happens to be true."

I knew how he felt.

When I became a Christian, I didn't give a great deal of thought to the consequences of deciding to follow Christ as my Lord and Saviour. I was overwhelmed by Christ's love for me in dying in my place and taking the punishment my sins deserved. The idea that I could be forgiven for everything—that was nearly too good to be true.

As time went by, I began to realize that not only was continuous forgiveness possible but that I had received the Holy Spirit to live with me. As I read the Bible, he began to teach me to readjust my thinking and to bring it in line with the way God was thinking. Sometimes this was painful, but it was also good. He began to make me into a person with a character just like the Lord Jesus Christ. I was thankful about that. Jesus is such an impressive person! He is so clean, so right, so kind and loving, so honest. I found, as time went by, that I longed more and more to be like him.

In addition to these things, I had a clear promise from the Bible that God would guide me each step along the way. At the time of making decisions, I was often uncertain which way to go but, looking back, I can see that God was guiding me and caring for me. It is always clearer in retrospect. What a joy that is!

When I went to church as a young Christian it was great. So many new friends—brothers and sisters in Christ. I had become a member of the family of God. I know that some people have had bad experiences at church. I am sorry about that, but that has not been my story. I have experienced love, kindness and care. I have always loved being with God's people because it gives me a chance to love them. When the Bible has been taught well, it has fed and exhorted me. I have enjoyed singing and praying with others, and drinking in the encouragement of simply being in the presence of forgiven people like me.

But probably the best thing of all about becoming a Christian was the promise that one day I would take my place in the everlasting new creation that Christ has prepared for his followers. I didn't realize this all at once. As time went by, it all seemed better than my best hope.

However, that is not the full picture. Right from the beginning, I also found living as a Christian much more difficult than I had imagined. It was one thing to say, "Lord Jesus, please take all of my life and use me in your service". It was entirely another thing to **do it**.

You see, up to the time of my conversion, I had thought and acted like the pagan I was. I thought the world existed for my pleasure. However, as a Christian man all that had to change. But change was slow and difficult. To my great disappointment, I had to learn the same lessons over and over again. The more I seemed to draw near to Christ, the more I recognized my need for change. This was sometimes painful.

Why, for example, was it so hard to read the Bible? I enjoyed it when I did it, but it took me so long to get around to doing it. I would think of urgent matters to attend to—a letter to write, a phone call to make. Matters were made worse when someone told me I shouldn't read it unless I really wanted to, in case it led to 'legalism' (whatever that was). Under this 'guidance', I stopped altogether. One day I said to myself, "Chappo, just do it! It must be better to do it even if you don't feel much like it, than not to read it at all." So I did, and it made a great deal of difference.

This could be repeated with my prayer life, evangelism, and other forms of Christian obedience. For example, I was now to be a careful steward of my time and money. They were to be brought under the authority of Christ and not squandered on self-indulgence.

In addition, I discovered that I was at odds with many of my former peers. They were not trying to follow Christ, and they didn't want me to either.

In the area of morality, I had to learn that people's lives were sacred and important. They were as much in need of help as I had been. I had been totally self-centred in the past, and I used people. That behaviour had to change. I was to be Christ-centred and consequently other-person centred, as he was. That remains a hard lesson to learn.

Sinful habits from the past dogged my footsteps. Some days I felt overwhelmed. It seemed an endless grind.

From time to time, well-meaning Christians offered me a 'cure' for my situation. I tried method after method in an endeavour to reach a higher, more successful plain of Christian living. These all turned out to be waterless springs. I was the same person.

The long and short of it is that I have reached the stage where I am happy to say that living the Christian life is both good—really good—but also hard. There is no way that I would ever opt out, but there is also no way that I am going to avoid the struggle. I have come to see that this is the normal way the Bible writers experienced the Christian life. And so it is for me.

This book is designed to help us see that this constant battle to live a life pleasing to God is not only normal but God's way of strengthening us and making us Christlike. Like a loving Father, God has his eye on us for good. His gracious purpose for us is that we live in the tension between longing for Christlikeness and being unable, this side of glory, to do that perfectly.

We are, in fact, people with a foot in two worlds. We have one foot firmly planted in this world and, at the same time, one foot planted in the world to come, where everything is perfect. This brings its own tension which cannot be totally relieved until Christ's return or when we go to be with him in death. However, this does not stop us from enjoying life with God now while we wait patiently for then.

What I aim to do in the following pages is describe how the Bible sees our present age, and also what the Bible says about the age to come. I will try and show how our simultaneous membership of both worlds brings us tension, and how the Bible envisages us living with this tension. I will also describe some counterfeit methods I have observed to relieve the tension, so we will not be easily deceived. And finally, I will look at some promises in God's word that have helped me. I hope they help you as well.

Chapter 2

THIS PRESENT WORLD

I WOKE WITH A START. I had slept through the alarm. It was late, and I was late for appointments. Words were spoken. Harsh words. Words spoken to me and by me. Too many words, in fact. I was glad when that day ended.

I was telling a friend about it and he said, "That's life!" How right he was. Life is often and exactly like that. It isn't always Murphy's Law but it certainly feels that way a lot of the time.[1]

Then again, this world is a great place to live in. There are so many beautiful places to visit, and so many clever and talented people who are fun to be

---

1   Murphy's Law: "If anything can go wrong, it will."

with, to say nothing of the beautiful things they create for our enjoyment.

Why is it like this—the good and the bad all mixed up together?

Good but fallen

In the first book of the Bible, we are told why our world is the way it is. Genesis begins with a description of God's creative activities. We read in chapter 1 that God spoke everything into being. He created everything from nothing. There is a recurring phrase after each act of creation: "And God saw that it was good".[2]

By the time we get to the end of chapter 2, God has created marriage. The man and his wife live harmoniously in God's garden, Eden. They "were both naked and were not ashamed".[3] They were totally honest and open with each other in a loving, caring relationship. What's more, they had a relationship with God himself. There was no discordant note at all. Even as I write this it is hard to believe. It seems so far away from reality. However, it didn't last.

By the time we get to the end of chapter 3, the wheel is off the bike totally. The man and his wife are

---

2   Genesis 1:10, 12, 18, 25, 31
3   Genesis 2:25

in a struggle to see who will be first. Their marriage is under threat. They are afraid of God and try to hide from him. The environment has become hostile to the man as he tends the garden, and work has become burdensome. What has happened?

When God placed the man and woman in the garden he also planted two special 'trees'. One was the tree of life. The symbolism is clear. If you ate its fruit you had eternal life. The man and the woman had free access to this tree. There was another tree called 'the tree of the knowledge of good and evil'. Eating its fruit was forbidden and a warning was placed on it. God said, "in the day that you eat of it you shall surely die".[4]

In the story, we are introduced to Satan in the form of a serpent. He tempts the woman to disobey God's clear command and eat the forbidden fruit. He uses a threefold deception. First, he tempts her to doubt God's word with his innuendo, "Did God actually say …?" He is suggesting that the command was not quite as she had been told. It is always flattering to think that we are in a position to correct God.

The second suggestion he makes to her is that there will be no consequences flowing from disobedience to God. "You will not surely die", he suggests to the woman.[5] He is saying in fact, "There is no judgement".

---

4   Genesis 2:17
5   Genesis 3:4-5

Many have fallen for that line.

The third suggestion, and the most appealing one of all, is that God does not have her best interest at heart and is in fact self-interested in the command. "God knows that when you eat of it your eyes will be opened, and you will be like God, knowing good and evil" is his suggestion. He is really suggesting that she will be God's equal. She will be able to say what is good and what is evil, which is God's prerogative. She will, in fact, be equal with God, judging as God does.

Like all the works of the devil, it is clever but a total lie. The woman falls for it, and so does Adam, and everything starts to come apart. The man and the woman vie for importance in leadership. What was harmonious before becomes competitive and jealous. Things deteriorate so badly that by the time we reach chapter 4 of Genesis we find that Cain has murdered his brother Abel.

Worse still, when God visits Adam and Eve in the garden, they are afraid of him and try to hide from him. They no longer want to be friends with him. The judgement of God falls on them as surely as night follows day. They are excluded from the garden, and in particular from the tree of life. They are doomed to die, just as God had said.

The situation would have been hopeless had not God, in his mercy, promised that he would ultimately reverse this 'fallenness' of the world through the seed of the woman. "He", said God to the serpent, "shall bruise your head".[6] This person is, of course, the Lord Jesus Christ, but that is the story of the rest of the Bible.

The opening chapters of Genesis show us why the good and the bad are mixed together in our world. Beautiful countrysides are destroyed by greedy people. Seemingly reliable people prove that they cannot be trusted. Marriages that start in love and optimism end in malice and despair.

I heard a boy say one day, "I'm always hurting the people I love most. Why am I twisted like that?" I knew just what he meant.

The history of the 20th century shows that we are not very good at living harmoniously with each other. What a field day historians will have describing the last century! It was the most advanced century in terms of technology, but also in terms of killing and bloodshed. Do you ever wonder if we will ever learn? I was horrified to hear on TV last week a religious leader from Iran saying that "the annihilation of Israel was inevitable". I am praying that he is wrong. Killing people is not a good option at all.

However, lest you think I have a jaundiced view of life, let me say I think this world is a wonderful place in which to live. I have been at the top of Niagara Falls in high spring. The tulips and magnolias were in full

---

6   Genesis 3:15

bloom and there was enough spray for a brilliant rainbow to form. I have been gobsmacked night after night at the wonderful sunsets in the western plains of New South Wales. I have been entertained for hours and hours by books and music written by brilliant people for my enjoyment. Sometimes these have been so beautiful I have been reduced to tears, or so amusing that I have rolled around in peals of laughter. But it isn't always like this!

I am not a passive onlooker in my world. I am an active participant. I am part of it and I find the good and bad mingled **in me**. Sometimes I surprise myself at some act of self-sacrifice. At other times, I am disturbed at how selfish I can be. I am not thoroughly bad but I am a very long way short of being thoroughly good. I am, to put it theologically, "made in the image of God, but fallen".

That's me and that's my world too. This fallenness can be described in other ways as well.

In the power of the Evil One

The Apostle John describes our world as being in the power of the "evil one".[7]

It is a great mistake to discount the existence of the

---

[7]   1 John 5:19

devil as if it were a 'primitive' way of accounting for evil in the world. I am reminded of the two boys discussing theology. One said to the other, "Do you believe in the devil?"

"No", said the other, "he is like Santa. It's really your father!"

Nothing could please the devil more than for us to disbelieve in his existence. Our age has tried to trivialize him. We depict him in an opera cape with an overgrown toasting fork. He always looks as if he is on his way to a fancy dress masquerade. No-one is worried by such a comical character.

But the devil is **not** like that.

The Lord Jesus spoke often about the devil. Sometimes he calls him "the ruler of this world".[8] Jesus says "he was a murderer from the beginning" and is "the father of lies".[9] He is by nature evil, and he is opposed to all of God's activities.[10] He persecutes Christian people and seeks their destruction. He is rightly called 'the destroyer'.[11] He is cunning and can sometimes disguise himself as "an angel of light".[12]

Is he to be feared? Yes! He is to be taken seriously and dealt with appropriately. In 1 Peter we are told to

---

[8]   John 12:31, 16:11
[9]   John 8:44
[10]   1 Peter 5:8
[11]   Revelation 9:11
[12]   2 Corinthians 11:14

resist him.[13] The Apostle Paul tells us to "put on the whole armour of God" so we can stand against the devil (but more of this later).[14] It might help us to think about the devil's activities so we can recognize them more easily.

He deludes us

The devil is a master of deception. What could be a greater delusion than to believe that if you hijacked a plane and flew it into the Twin Towers in New York, with all the attendant carnage, that you would go straight to paradise? Those men are not now in paradise. They were deluded. In temples in Japan, you can have your fortune told by paying for a small bird to pick up a scrap of paper in the bottom of the bird's cage. What a delusion! In the Western world, the devil's great deception is to cause us to believe that we can live perfectly happy lives while ignoring God completely. Somehow or other we have been conned into believing that all will be well in the end, and that there is no judgement day and no hell at all. This is a total delusion. He may have suggested to you that sinning doesn't matter very much because you can be easily forgiven. He is deluding you. It does matter.

---

[13] 1 Peter 5:9
[14] Ephesians 6:10ff

He discourages us

The devil sows the seed in our minds that we will never be any good as Christians. He suggests that to give up in our struggle is easier that struggling against sin in our lives and in the world. Don't listen to him. He is a liar. He is trying to discourage you. In Jesus' parable of the soils, it is Satan who snatches away the seed from people lest they get converted.[15]

One of the ways the devil discourages us is to isolate us from our fellow Christians, perhaps by persuading us that they are all better than we are and that we should stay away from them until we can get our act together. We are all like each other in our struggle to be Christlike. Don't listen to the devil. He is a liar.

He denounces us

Having tempted us to sin, the devil then proceeds to denounce us for being sinners. He is no gentleman. He is wicked through and through. You can see him in action in the early chapters of Job. Job is a good and upright man, and Satan suggests to God that he is only so because God has been kind to him. Job has a lovely family and great wealth. Satan suggests that if Job were to lose his family, wealth and health he would

---

15 Mark 4:15

not be godly at all. This happens in a terrible accident, but Job remains faithful. (You can read it for yourself in the opening chapter of the book of Job.)

One of the meanings of the word 'Satan' is 'the accuser'. This is why the message of Romans 8 is such good news. The question is asked, "Who shall bring any charge against God's elect?", and the implicit answer is "No-one!"[16] This is because, as Revelation reminds us, "the salvation and the power and the kingdom of our God and the authority of his Christ have come, for the accuser of our brothers has been thrown down, who accuses them day and night before our God".[17]

He diverts us

Another of Satan's evil ways is to divert Christians from following the Lord Jesus wholeheartedly. He offers us alternatives to following the path of obedience. Sometimes he suggests a course of action which isn't of itself wrong but is less than helpful. He causes us to think we will be happy if we acquire enough 'toys'. I saw on a t-shirt the words, "He who dies with the most toys wins". But of course he who dies with the most toys still dies!

---

[16]   Romans 8:33
[17]   Revelation 12:10

Don't let the devil distract you. That was the mistake of the rich fool in the famous parable. You will remember that the man works hard and acquires enough money to retire. The trouble is he dies that day. He has no time to enjoy his wealth, and what's worse he finds himself unready to meet God. "Fool" is the word God uses to describe him.[18]

I once heard someone say that we have to give full expression to our potential. I have lived a full life; I've had three different careers (and enjoyed them all) and travelled extensively around the world. But it is impossible to give full expression to my potential. I am made in the image of God. I have hardly scratched the surface of making the most of my potential. I will need eternity for that.

It's easy to be diverted from the single-minded pursuit of Christlikeness of character, even by the subtle temptation to 'fulfil our potential'.

His demise is sure

When Jesus died and rose again from the dead he paid the price our sins deserve. He sacrificed himself in our place in an act of self-giving love.[19] This action not only secured salvation for us but it also nullified the

---

18 Luke 12:20
19 John 3:16

power of the devil to destroy us. Jesus came to destroy the works of the devil.[20]

Satan may appear powerful but he exercises his power under God's permission.[21] His ultimate destruction is assured.[22]

This world: a perfect environment for sinners

It isn't possible to live in our world and not be conscious that all is not well, unless you pretend. Internationally we cannot live at peace with each other. In my lifetime I have witnessed the Second World War with all of its horror, Korea, Vietnam, Northern Ireland, Bosnia, Kenya, the Sudan and the Middle East (and I'm sure there are others I have left out)—not to mention the brutality of oppressive regimes like those in Russia, China, Uganda, Cambodia and Argentina.

What is clear internationally is repeated nationally, and in family life and in local communities. In my homeland, I have been burgled three times. In the end, to get insurance, I had a security system like Fort Knox. One in three marriages in Australia ends in

---

[20] 1 John 3:8; John 12:30-33
[21] Job 1
[22] Revelation 20:10

divorce. This leads me to believe we aren't all that good at living with each other.

All of the above are warning signs. They say, "All is not well". They should stimulate the question, "What has gone wrong?" Surely it wasn't meant to be like this! It cries out for a solution, and we should be searching for that solution.

However, if we lived in a world where everything went along harmoniously, and if we were to all 'live happily ever afterwards', do you think we would seek after God? I doubt it! God has allowed our world to 'fall apart' in order to warn us and prompt us to turn back to him. The world keeps shouting at us: "All is not well!"

Now I don't want to suggest for a moment that I am an innocent bystander in this world. I am an active participant. What can be writ large about the world can also be said of me in a smaller measure. I am a child of my age. I am, at heart, a rebel against God. I have said "no" to Jesus Christ as ruler of my life.[23] Like the woman in the garden of Eden, I too have listened to the lying voice of the devil. I too have said, "I will be god over me", and echoed the one who said, "I am the master of my life, the captain of my soul". I am not innocent.[24]

---

[23] Ephesians 2:2
[24] Ephesians 2:3

We SEE, THEN, IN THE WORLD and within ourselves, both good and bad. I am made in God's image but fallen. I was made for better things. However, left to my own devices, I am subject to God's judgement and under his wrath, just like everyone else.

Only God can change this condition. Without Christ's help I would have chosen to remain a rebel because that was what I wanted to do. I was rightly described as a slave to sin and death. I always said "no" to Christ.

God, in his kindness, has made that change. He has enabled me to say "yes" to Jesus. And he has given me his Holy Spirit.[25]

This is my world. The world into which I was born; the world in which I laugh and cry; the world in which I will die. While it is good, it isn't good enough. I am meant to be dissatisfied. Thankfully, that isn't all there is.

---

[25] Ephesians 1:11-14

Chapter 3

THE WORLD TO COME: THE NEW CREATION

Jesus began his earthly ministry by announcing that this world isn't all that there will be. Something wonderful was coming, and soon: "the kingdom of God".[1] When Jesus taught the disciples about the kingdom in the parables, it was clear that he was the king of God's kingdom. As Jesus moved through his world, it was also very clear from his behaviour that he was that king. He cast out demons, healed the sick, raised the dead, fed the hungry, stilled the storm at sea, and brought calm to the lives of distraught men

---

[1]   Mark 1:14-15

and women whose problems were solved one after the other. The supreme act of his kingly power was to die a sin-bearing death on the cross and rise again from the dead as the great conqueror of death.

All this was for us. In this action, Jesus was not only able to forgive us but set us free from serving our master, the devil.[2] In union with Christ, we are declared righteous, and free from all accusation and condemnation. In his resurrection from the dead, Jesus showed that he had defeated Satan decisively.

All the same, in this world here and now Satan is not totally destroyed, nor has the kingdom come in all its fullness and freedom. Jesus' kingdom is recognized by people of faith, but it will not be until the next world that faith will give way to sight. When the new creation comes, everyone will know and recognize that Jesus is the rightful ruler in God's kingdom,[3] and Satan and all evil will be done away with completely and permanently.[4] It is almost impossible to contemplate how wonderful that will be.

---

[2]   John 12:30-33; Hebrews 2:14-15
[3]   Revelation 22:3-4
[4]   Revelation 20:10, 21:7-8

An environment perfect for holy people

In a glorious picture in the last book of the Bible, John tells us that he saw a vast, innumerable crowd of people from every nation and tribe of the earth. These people had "washed their robes and made them white in the blood of the Lamb".[5]

This is what it will be like in the new creation that Christ is preparing for his people. Only the redeemed will belong there—only those who have been washed, forgiven and made new through the work of the Lord Jesus in dying and rising to life for them.

In this new creation, no stain of sin will remain. Through the work of the Holy Spirit, we will be perfected in character. We will, in fact, be just like the Lord Jesus himself.[6] We will be as God intended us to be when he said, "Let us make man in our image".[7] That work, which is gradual and partial in this life, will be miraculously brought to completion when we take our place in the new creation.[8]

When the Bible writers describe the new creation, it is often in poetry. In Isaiah 11, there is a wonderful poem about the Messiah and what he will finally do:

---

[5]   Revelation 7:9-17
[6]   1 John 3:1-3
[7]   Genesis 1:26
[8]   1 John 3:2-3

... He shall not judge by what his eyes see,
    or decide disputes by what his ears hear,
but with righteousness he shall judge the poor,
    and decide with equity for the meek of the earth;
and he shall strike the earth with the rod of his mouth,
    and with the breath of his lips he shall kill the wicked.
Righteousness shall be the belt of his waist,
    and faithfulness the belt of his loins.

The wolf shall dwell with the lamb,
    and the leopard shall lie down with the young goat,
and the calf and the lion and the fattened calf together;
    and a little child shall lead them.
The cow and the bear shall graze;
    their young shall lie down together;
    and the lion shall eat straw like the ox.
The nursing child shall play over the hole of the cobra,
    and the weaned child shall put his hand on the
        adder's den.
They shall not hurt or destroy
    in all my holy mountain ... (Isa 11:3-9)

This is very good news for the lamb, the goat and the cow—to say nothing of the mother of the little child! It is like the garden of Eden all over again. Nothing hurts, nothing destroys. People now have free access to the tree of life again.[9]

---

[9]   Revelation 22:14

In the New Testament there is another prose-poem about the new creation:

> Then I saw a new heaven and a new earth, for the first heaven and the first earth had passed away, and the sea was no more. And I saw the holy city, new Jerusalem, coming down out of heaven from God, prepared as a bride adorned for her husband. And I heard a loud voice from the throne saying, "Behold, the dwelling place of God is with man. He will dwell with them, and they will be his people, and God himself will be with them as their God. He will wipe away every tear from their eyes, and death shall be no more, neither shall there be mourning, nor crying, nor pain any more, for the former things have passed away."
>
> And he who was seated on the throne said, "Behold, I am making all things new." (Rev 21:1-5)

What a wonderful place that will be! There will be no more tears; no sorrow; no death; no parting. What a beautiful picture: God "will wipe away every tear from their eyes". I know that this is poetry, but don't let that blind us to the reality. What Jesus did on earth for a few years and for just a few people, he will do for the whole creation. He will heal it and set it free. He has shown that he can do it, and he will do it because of his promise. There will be no more locks on doors; no more fear of walking at night; no more loneliness; no more pain (which is very good news indeed for back sufferers and the arthritic); no more cancer; no more harsh and angry words. It is a perfect environment for holy people, which is what we will be. We, too, will fit perfectly into this world because our holiness, for which we have been striving, will have been brought to completion.[10] We will have a resurrection body just as Jesus has a resurrection body.

The Bible writers are anxious to get there:

> For to me to live is Christ, and to die is gain. If I am
> to live in the flesh, that means fruitful labour for
> me. Yet which I shall choose I cannot tell. I am hard
> pressed between the two. My desire is to depart and
> be with Christ, for that is far better. But to remain
> in the flesh is more necessary on your account.
> (Phil 1:21-24)

I sometimes wonder if we have forgotten how really good it will be. If we were debating which we would choose, I rather suspect we would cling to this life at all costs.

Universal peace for all nations

This world can rightly be described as a place of "wars and rumours of wars",[11] but in the new creation there will be no more wars. There will be universal peace.

---

[10] 1 John 3:1-3
[11] Matthew 24:6

There will be no need to seek for justice. Everyone will deal fairly. This will happen person to person, people to people, nation to nation. Look at this lovely poem of Isaiah:

> It shall come to pass in the latter days
>   that the mountain of the house of the LORD
> shall be established as the highest of the mountains,
>   and shall be lifted up above the hills;
> and all the nations shall flow to it,
>   and many peoples shall come, and say:
> "Come, let us go up to the mountain of the LORD,
>   to the house of the God of Jacob,
> that he may teach us his ways
>   and that we may walk in his paths."
> For out of Zion shall go the law,
>   and the word of the LORD from Jerusalem.
> He shall judge between the nations,
>   and shall decide disputes for many peoples;
> and they shall beat their swords into plowshares,
>   and their spears into pruning hooks;
> nation shall not lift up sword against nation,
>   neither shall they learn war anymore.
>
> O house of Jacob,
>   come, let us walk
>   in the light of the LORD. (Isa 2:2-5)

Can you imagine what a world it will be?

In a similar vein the writer of the last book of the Bible describes the new creation this way:

After this I looked, and behold, a great multitude that no one could number, from every nation, from all tribes and peoples and languages, standing before the throne and before the Lamb, clothed in white robes, with palm branches in their hands, and crying out with a loud voice, "Salvation belongs to our God who sits on the throne, and to the Lamb!" And all the angels were standing around the throne and around the elders and the four living creatures, and they fell on their faces before the throne and worshiped God, saying, "Amen! Blessing and glory and wisdom and thanksgiving and honor and power and might be to our God forever and ever! Amen." (Rev 7:9-12)

Did you notice they were from every tribe and nation —all together—caught up in the wonder of service to their king? At last the curse of the Tower of Babel is reversed.[12] They are no longer scattered—no longer confused by language—but all one in the new creation.

Here and now is not all there is. By far the best is yet to come. The new creation is described as "coming down out of heaven".[13] We do not make heaven on earth. God is creating a new world—a fitting place for God's people to be with him forever. Do not doubt that this will take place. Jesus has promised it.

---

[12] Genesis 11:1-9
[13] Revelation 21:1-3

Chapter 4

A FOOT IN TWO WORLDS

CHRISTIAN PEOPLE HAVE A foot in two worlds. They are children of this world with all its highs and lows, its temptations and failures, its good times and bad. And they have become children of the age to come, with all its glories and blessings. This is well described in Ephesians 2:

> And you were dead in the trespasses and sins in which you once walked, following the course of this world, following the prince of the power of the air, the spirit that is now at work in the sons of disobedience—among whom we all once lived in the passions of our flesh, carrying out the desires of the body and the mind, and were by nature children of wrath, like the rest of mankind. But God, being rich in mercy, because of the great love with which

he loved us, even when we were dead in our
trespasses, made us alive together with Christ—by
grace you have been saved—and raised us up with
him and seated us with him in the heavenly places
in Christ Jesus, so that in the coming ages he might
show the immeasurable riches of his grace in
kindness toward us in Christ Jesus. (Eph 2:1-7)

Did you notice that we are **already** seated with Christ in
the heavenly realms? I'm not sure that I fully understand what this means. It is certainly saying that I am
in Christ. He is seated in the heavenly realms because
of his victory over sin and death, and so in some sense
I am also seated in heaven because I am "in Christ".
When I became a Christian, I became a member of
both worlds simultaneously. This is according to the
promise in John 3:16:

"For God so loved the world, that he gave his only
Son, that whoever believes in him should not perish
but have eternal life."

Now, in one sense, this wonderful promise of eternal
life is our hope for the future. It belongs to the age to
come, as Jesus says in Luke 18:30. It is a sure and
certain hope, and we look forward to inheriting it when
we die or when Jesus returns, whichever comes first.
However, the promise is not just for then but for now.
When a person believes in the Lord Jesus Christ then
that person **has** eternal life, starting here and now. As
Jesus says a few chapters later in John's Gospel: "Truly,

truly I say to you, whoever believes has eternal life".[1] Or as John puts it in his first letter: "I write these things to you who believe in the name of the Son of God that you may know that you have eternal life".[2]

Christians have eternal life as a present possession, starting from when they believed in Christ. If you were brought up always believing in Christ, you may not remember exactly when this took place. In my case, I remember the day and the place very clearly, so life-changing was it.

The Holy Spirit—our helper and guarantee

However, that's not all. Not only was I forgiven when I turned to Christ, and given eternal life, and made a member of God's family, but I was also given the Holy Spirit as a down payment of the new creation to come. This is the promise of Ephesians 1:13-14:

> In him you also, when you heard the word of truth, the gospel of your salvation, and believed in him, were sealed with the promised Holy Spirit, who is the guarantee of our inheritance until we acquire possession of it, to the praise of his glory.

---

[1]   John 6:47
[2]   1 John 5:13

The Holy Spirit is God dwelling with and in us. He works with and in us, making us Christlike people in our character and our actions. It is not possible to be a real Christian and not to have the Holy Spirit. It was the Holy Spirit who empowered us to say "Yes" to Jesus as our Lord and Saviour in the first place. Prior to the Spirit's work, we always said "No" to the challenge of the gospel. Our wills were crippled by the fall, and we needed help to overcome their downward pull. Prior to the Spirit's work, we did as we liked, and what we liked was completely contrary to following Jesus.

The gift of the Holy Spirit is an astonishing act of God's grace, enabling us to respond to his word, and reassuring us that we do indeed have a guaranteed place in the world to come. However, the Spirit's presence immediately puts us into conflict with the powers that be in this world.

The world, the flesh and the devil

At age seven I was attending Sunday School at St Paul's, Oatley, in New South Wales. While children of my age all over the world were learning to recite Bible verses, I was learning to recite the church's catechism!

I well remember saying: "My godfathers and godmothers promised that ... I would renounce the devil and all his works, the vain pomp and vanity of this wicked world and all the sinful lusts of the flesh".

I hadn't the faintest idea what "the vain pomp and vanity of this wicked world" was, but about ten years later I had inklings. As for the "sinful lusts of the flesh", I was clueless. But I knew well enough by the time I got to my middle teens (but not by that name)!

These are, nonetheless, a good summary of the powers and forces which pull against all Christians: the world, the flesh and the devil. All three are real and important, and work against us. In fact, a very common mistake is to so emphasize one of these as to make the other two drift into the background and all but disappear.

For example, if we overly concentrate on the devil, we will tend to blame all our difficulties on him. A young man told me once that he thought he was demon-possessed. When I asked why he thought this, he told me that he was always thinking lustful thoughts. I explained that this was the flesh, not a demon. He didn't need to be exorcised; he needed to learn how to deal with the flesh (more of this later). Because of his over-emphasis on the devil, he had neglected the flesh and so sought a less than satisfactory solution to his problem.

Let me see if I can describe what the world, the flesh and the devil are, and how they should be dealt with.

The world

There are three ways in which the term 'world' is used in the New Testament. The context will tell you which one is being referred to. First, it can refer to the earth on which we live, as in Psalm 24:1: "The earth is the LORD's and the fullness thereof, the world and those who dwell therein".

Second, the term 'world' can be used for all the people who live in the world, as in John 3:16: "For God so loved the world, that he gave his only Son, that whoever believes in him should not perish but have eternal life".

However, 'the world' has a third meaning and that is the one in which we are interested. We are warned not to love the world or the things in the world.[3] Such love will replace our love for the Father. But what does it mean to "love the world"? John goes on to define it:

> For all that is in the world—the desires of the flesh and
> the desires of the eyes and pride in possessions—is not
> from the Father but is from the world. And the world
> is passing away along with its desires, but whoever
> does the will of God abides forever. (1 John 2:16-17)

This is a broad definition. It encompasses everything that is sinful: a love for self-gratification; giving in to the cravings of our sinful natures; wanting everything we see (which leads to covetousness and idolatry);

---

[3]   1 John 2:15

being captivated by beauty as if God were not its author; and pride in self-achievement and possessions.

The foolishness of being a slave to these things is that they are passing away. I think it can be best described as thinking about our lives as if God were not there and as if I was the centre of my universe. It is like being captivated by the wonder of the sunset yet not recognizing that God made it for our enjoyment.

It is very possible to be a Christian and still adopt the attitudes of the 'world'. We live in the same sorts of houses as everyone else; we take the same holidays; our aspirations for our children seem very like the pagan world around us—we want our children to have lucrative professions, and are horrified when they announce that they want to serve in low-paid jobs as teachers, development workers or missionaries. We view retirement as a holiday and, apart from going to church on Sunday, our lifestyle seems no different from everyone else's. It is very easy to slip into thinking like everyone else in the world around us. This is why John warns us not to love the world and all that is in it, and why Jesus also tells us to take care:

> Therefore do not be anxious, saying, 'What shall we eat?' or 'What shall we drink?' or 'What shall we wear?' For the Gentiles seek after all these things, and your heavenly Father knows that you need them all. But seek first the kingdom of God and his righteousness, and all these things will be added to you. (Matt 6:31-33)

How can this be overcome? The Bible tells us we need a renewed mind. See how this is described in Romans 12:1-2:

> I appeal to you therefore, brothers, by the mercies of God, to present your bodies as a living sacrifice, holy and acceptable to God, which is your spiritual worship. Do not be conformed to this world, but be transformed by the renewal of your mind, that by testing you may discern what is the will of God, what is good and acceptable and perfect.

JB Phillips's famous paraphrase of this passage says: "Don't let the world around you squeeze you into its own mould, but let God re-mould your minds from within".[4] This renewing is a gracious work of the Holy Spirit. As we read our Bibles, he helps us to readjust our thinking so that we think the Bible's thoughts. This is another way of saying that we start to think God's thoughts after him. Little by little, our minds are made to think like Christ's. We are no longer 'conned' by the spirit of our age. The advertisers use ever more sophisticated methods to persuade me that I really do need a new TV, even though my current one is fine. In my best moments, I see through it and resist. In my worst moments, I am as acquisitive as everyone else. Only

---

[4]   JB Phillips, *Letters to Young Churches*, Geoffrey Bles, London, 1947, p. 27.

the Holy Spirit can help us to get our minds straight. The renewed mind is the answer to worldliness.

The flesh

The word 'flesh' can mean our physical bodies, such as flesh and bones. It can also be a synonym for being human. But it is also used in the Bible as a term for the sinful, rebellious part of our nature, which has come to us because of the fall. The 'flesh' in this sense can lead us to sin by misusing our physical desires.

For example, our desire for food is good and God-given, but it is easy for that to be misused and become gluttony (with obesity and all its problems to follow). Sleep is good and necessary, but laziness is sinful. Sex is pleasurable and powerful when used properly in marriage to bind relationships; when misused it can have devastating effects. Human relationships are great when there is love and respect; when people are used and manipulated, it can be destructive. The works of the flesh are described this way in Galatians:

> Now the works of the flesh are evident: sexual immorality, impurity, sensuality, idolatry, sorcery, enmity, strife, jealousy, fits of anger, rivalries, dissensions, divisions, envy, drunkenness, orgies, and things like these. I warn you, as I warned you before, that those who do such things will not inherit the kingdom of God. (Gal 5:19-21)

Paul says that the normal Christian life will always involve conflict and tension, because there is a spiritual war raging inside of us—a battle between the "desires of the flesh" and the "desires of the Spirit":

> For the desires of the flesh are against the Spirit,
> and the desires of the Spirit are against the flesh,
> for these are opposed to each other, to keep you
> from doing the things you want to do. (Gal 5:17)

The desires of the 'flesh' and the 'Spirit' are completely incompatible, even though they are both located in our bodies. We now have God's Spirit and want to become more like Christ, and yet sinful desires remain active within us.

The great 17th-century Christian teacher John Owen used the image of a forest to describe these two principles or desires at work within us. Before we become Christians, sin has completely free reign in our lives. Sin is like a dense forest, where the ground is completely covered by trees, vines and undergrowth. No light can break in, and there is no opposing power or principle to stand in sin's way.

When the powerful work of God through the gospel breaks into a person's life, there is now a new principle, a new power at work—God's own Spirit. Some trees are uprooted, others are pruned, and light streams in. The condemnation due to sin is dealt with by Christ's blood, and the dominion or rule of sin is broken. A new master has claimed ownership, and the dense forest begins to be beaten back. Here and there, clearings begin to appear as aspects of a person's life are changed.

However, the forest remains. Large tracts of it may be quite untouched. What is more, the forest is still alive. It will not wither and die on its own. In fact, it will seek to take back the cleared land if it can.

With the help and power of the Holy Spirit, Christians are to work at clearing the land in two ways. The first is to be obedient to the Holy Spirit, and to follow his lead in becoming more like Christ. In Galatians 5:22ff we are told what the results of this will look like:

> But the fruit of the Spirit is love, joy, peace, patience, kindness, goodness, faithfulness, gentleness, self-control; against such things there is no law. And those who belong to Christ Jesus have crucified the flesh with its passions and desires.
>
> If we live by the Spirit, let us also walk by the Spirit. (Gal 5:22-25)

We are not surprised to see that the fruits of the Spirit are Christlike characteristics—remember, Christ had the Spirit without measure. These godly attributes are to be actively pursued, longed for, prayed for.

If the first remedy is to actively walk by the Spirit, the second is to actively resist and kill the desires of the flesh. In another of his letters, Paul puts it like this:

> Put to death therefore what is earthly in you: sexual immorality, impurity, passion, evil desire, and covetousness, which is idolatry. On account of these

the wrath of God is coming. In these you too once walked, when you were living in them. But now you must put them all away: anger, wrath, malice, slander, and obscene talk from your mouth. Do not lie to one another, seeing that you have put off the old self with its practices. (Col 3:5-9)

When we became Christians, we turned our back on an old way of life which was marked by self-indulgence. We turned towards a new way of life which was Christ-oriented and marked by obedience. Now, says Paul, we must keep hacking away at the vines and bushes and trees that belong to our former lives, and which now deceive and distract us from living like Christ.

This happens through the renewing of our minds, as we prayerfully read and listen to the word of God.

The devil

Back to the catechism: "my godfathers and godmothers promised that ... I would renounce the devil and all his works". I have described the activities and person of the devil in a previous chapter, but I need to say something about how to combat him and his temptations. He will try to get us to sin by whatever means he can. He will try to activate our 'flesh', and tempt us with aspects of the world.

The Bible tells us how to deal with the devil:

> Be sober-minded; be watchful. Your adversary the
> devil prowls around like a roaring lion, seeking
> someone to devour. Resist him, firm in your faith,
> knowing that the same kinds of suffering are being
> experienced by your brotherhood throughout the
> world. (1 Pet 5:8-9)

Please notice what God tells us to do. We are not to
cave in at every suggestion the devil makes. He is not
our master any more. He does not have to be obeyed.
When temptation comes into our minds, we are to
recognize its origin. "That idea", you say, "is dredged
up from the pit", and then you boot it out.

The renewed mind comes into play here in helping
us to recognize temptation for what it is. "I know your
tricky and twisted ways", we say. "I have no part with
you." We resist him.

Another Bible passage which has helped me is
James 4:7-8a:

> Submit yourselves therefore to God. Resist the
> devil, and he will flee from you. Draw near to God,
> and he will draw near to you.

This is a promise full of assurance. If we resist the devil
he will flee from us, and if we draw near to God he will
draw near to us. We are not alone in this struggle.

In addition to resisting, we are told in Ephesians 6
to put on the whole armour of God so that when the
devil comes to us, we will be able to resist him and
stand firm when he attacks:

Therefore take up the whole armour of God, that you may be able to withstand in the evil day, and having done all, to stand firm. Stand therefore, having fastened on the belt of truth, and having put on the breastplate of righteousness, and, as shoes for your feet, having put on the readiness given by the gospel of peace. In all circumstances take up the shield of faith, with which you can extinguish all the flaming darts of the evil one; and take the helmet of salvation, and the sword of the Spirit, which is the word of God, praying at all times in the Spirit, with all prayer and supplication. (Eph 6:13-18a)

It's called the armour of God not only because it comes from God, but because it's the armour that God himself puts on when he goes to war against his enemies (see Isaiah 59:17).

I have described the world, the flesh and the devil separately but in reality they are all intertwined. The devil is behind all temptations and sin. He will use any means to destroy us. The solutions are also intertwined. The renewed mind will help in every area of temptation, as well as instructing us in all good works. Putting on the whole armour of God, as we will see, will not only help us to resist the devil, but also to combat the world and the flesh.

Strenuous effort

Needless to say, all this requires strenuous effort. It would be good if we could all just take a 'holiness pill' and be instantly Christlike, but it just doesn't work like that.

Paul tells us that in his ministry of trying to present every person mature in Christ he toils, "struggling with all [Christ's] energy that he powerfully works within me".[5] This should be a great encouragement to us. He laboured and struggled just as we do. It wasn't easy at all. He wasn't empowered in such a way that he found it easy. To the contrary, he experienced God's power at work **because he didn't give up**. It was the exact opposite to what we might have thought.

Paul also describes the Christian life as a race. He says:

> ... that I may know him and the power of his
> resurrection, and may share his sufferings,
> becoming like him in his death, that by any means
> possible I may attain the resurrection from the dead.
>
> Not that I have already obtained this or am already
> perfect, but I press on to make it my own, because
> Christ Jesus has made me his own. Brothers, I do not
> consider that I have made it my own. But one thing I
> do: forgetting what lies behind and straining forward
> to what lies ahead, I press on toward the goal for the
> prize of the upward call of God in Christ Jesus. Let

---

5   Colossians 1:28-29

those of us who are mature think this way, and if in anything you think otherwise, God will reveal that also to you. (Phil 3:10-15)

Did you notice how he described maturity? He has not yet attained his goal (to know Christ fully), but he presses on to that end. This requires effort on his part. He is always "straining forward" so that he might "press on toward the goal". In much the same way, earlier in the letter Paul urged the Philippians to "work out your own salvation with fear and trembling, for it is God who works in you, both to will and to work for his good pleasure".[6]

This strenuous effort must always continue while ever we are still in this world. There are obstacles and forces and enemies that try to prevent us being Christlike. However, we have the Holy Spirit, who comes to our aid every step of the way.

Not only is there a tension inherent in Christian living, but our changing circumstances of life present us with new challenges and opportunities for growth. Take the young man who is converted in his teens. Among other things, he has to learn how a Christian son behaves towards his parents. That relationship will change when he marries. He must now learn to relate to them as a married man and to his wife as a Christian husband. In time he will have to learn to be a Christian father—then

---

[6]   Philippians 2:12b-13

how to relate to his children when they are adults. And then he will become a grandfather. Each stage brings new challenges and joys.

Keeping our eyes on Jesus

In all the changing circumstances of life, our Christlike aspirations will never be matched by our performance. There will always be tension. This is normal. We should learn to be thankful in this tension, because it is the God-given way to lead us to maturity as we fix our minds on Jesus, who is our goal. We would do well to concentrate on our hope of perfection, and how much we have been loved by the Lord Jesus Christ,[7] rather than be fixated with our fallenness.

This is the advice offered by the writer to the Hebrews:

> ... let us run with endurance the race that is set before us, looking to Jesus, the founder and perfecter of our faith, who for the joy that was set before him endured the cross, despising the shame, and is seated at the right hand of the throne of God.
>
> Consider him who endured from sinners such hostility against himself, so that you may not grow weary or fainthearted. (Heb 12:1b-3)

---

[7]   Romans 5:1-5

We find this difficult. Our age is very materialistic, and we are so taken up with all its pleasures and opportunities that we often neglect to think about the age to come. We tend to forget that this is not our ultimate home.[8]

For Paul, there was a gap between the perfection of the new creation, for which he longed, and his performance in this life. That gap will always exist, and we must accept it, even as we long for it to be closed. We must learn to be content with the dissatisfaction of not yet being what we one day will be.

---

8   Philippians 3:20-21

Chapter 5

RELIEVING THE TENSION

For as long as I have been a Christian, which has been more than 60 years, people have been offering me ways to relieve the tension caused by my membership of both this world and the world to come. On each occasion, some well-meaning Christian has told me of an easier way to live the Christian life than the continuous 'pressing on' that I have been describing. In each case, I was told that I could have the blessings of the new creation **now**.[1]

---

[1]   Technically this is known as 'realized eschatology'. Eschatology is the study of the 'last things', such as the return of the Lord Jesus, the final judgement, and the new creation. 'Realized eschatology' attempts to 'realize' or obtain now what actually belongs to the new creation.

Let me describe some of them so you can be on your guard.

Entire sanctification

I was converted at the age of 17. I had been a regular church-goer prior to that, but my active following of Jesus began in my late teens. Soon after my conversion, I came in contact with some fine Christian people who taught me that it was possible to have continuous victory over temptation in this life. It is important to note that they did **not** say I would be sinless. Had they done so, I would have immediately recognized the error. However, what they did offer was very close to it, a level of sanctification[2] that was almost complete, and I found it irresistible. It met the longing of my heart. How I yearned for that continuous victory over sin. They led me to believe that they had attained this state, and I had no cause to doubt them.

They taught me from Romans 6:11 that I was to consider myself "dead to sin and alive to God". The Lord Jesus had died to sin and I was to die to sin also.

---

[2] 'Sanctification' means to 'make holy'. It is often used to describe the ongoing process in the Christian life of becoming like Christ. The teaching that there is a way to be almost entirely free of sin in this life, and to live in victory over temptation, is often called 'entire sanctification'.

This meant that when temptation came, I was not to fight against it but to remember that I had died to sin, and then trust Christ to keep me free from sin.

Please don't misunderstand me. These were good and godly people. They were mistaken in their understanding of the Scriptures, but there was no doubting their desire to live holy lives. Like me, they longed to be like Christ, and I don't doubt that they had reached a higher plain of Christian obedience in their lives, but their understanding of what had happened to them was incorrect.

This teaching had a devastating effect on my Christian life. Rather than making me impervious to temptation, the result was that I rocketed into sin faster than ever. I did not resist the devil as I should have. This was very disappointing for me, and filled me with doubts. My peers claimed that it had worked for them, and since I didn't want to be the odd man out, I pretended that I was 'in the victory way' as well.

Eventually, in the providence of God, I was moved away from that fellowship. I determined that there was no future for me in lying to myself. I would tell the truth about my condition and seek, from the Bible, a better understanding of the way of growing in Christ-likeness.

What I discovered was that Romans 6:10-11 meant that Christ died to the **penalty** of sin—not the possibility of sin—and this was how I was to think about myself. I had also died to the penalty of sin through

Christ. I was no longer condemned. I was not going to be punished, because Christ had taken that for me.

In response to Christ's work, and by the power of his Spirit living in me, I was now to walk in a new life of obedience. I was to grow in Christlikeness in the way we explored in the previous chapter—positively by bringing forth the fruit of the Spirit, and negatively by putting to death the desires of the flesh.

Please take note what this teaching about entire sanctification did. In essence, it offered me the new creation now. No wonder it was irresistible. Had I studied my Bible with greater care I would have known better than to fall for it.

When I look back on these events, I think the most disturbing feature was that it divided the Christian community into the 'haves' and the 'have nots'. There were those who understood the secret of 'victorious Christian living', and there were the rest, who just battled on. However, the Bible doesn't make such a separation. In the Scriptures, a person is either "in Christ" or he isn't. And if we are "in Christ", we are united with each other, and are to urge and help each other to keep growing in Christlike character.

Charismatic movement

When I first encountered the Charismatic movement, I found that it also taught a two-tier system of sanctification. The difference was in how we received the Holy Spirit. It was taught that a believer could have the Holy Spirit and yet not be 'baptized with the Holy Spirit'. This was argued from the life of the early followers of the Lord Jesus. They had received the Holy Spirit when the resurrected Lord Jesus appeared to them, breathed on them and said, "Receive the Holy Spirit".[3] However, it was argued, they were not yet **baptized** with the Holy Spirit—that followed later at Pentecost.[4] This sounded reasonable on the surface, but not on closer investigation.

First: the disciples are examples to us in many ways, but in the way they related to God they were unique. They began as Old Testament believers. They met Jesus and became followers. They knew him 'in the flesh'. And after he ascended into heaven, they knew him by the Holy Spirit. There is a real sense in which they were not 'proper' disciples until the day of Pentecost. The position they finally arrived at was the position we started at, as Peter points out at the end of his Pentecost sermon.[5] What they had finally received at Pentecost we also received when we believed in the Lord Jesus Christ.

Second: it is never wise to try to harmonize the Gospels. If God had meant us to have one Gospel he

---

[3] John 20:22

[4] Acts 2

[5] Acts 2:38-39

wouldn't have given us four. Each Gospel is to be read as a complete work. In John's Gospel, for example, we are told early on that Jesus will baptize his followers with the Holy Spirit.[6] And I would expect this to happen before John finishes his Gospel. This does, in fact, happen when the resurrected Jesus breathes on his disciples and says "Receive the Holy Spirit". It is an acted parable of the coming of the Holy Spirit at Pentecost (which John doesn't describe at all). John has already introduced us to the idea of acted parables. When Jesus washed the disciple's feet, he said it was of greater significance than they realized. It was an acted parable of Jesus' death for them.[7] What happened in John 20 is an acted parable of what will happen at Pentecost. (Luke, whose account is much longer, recounts the events at Pentecost in detail. He does not describe the event in John 20. And neither gospeller records both events.)

Third: let me state again what seems to be the New Testament perspective. People are "in Christ" or they are not. If they are, they will long to have victory over sin, but will not experience that victory until the new creation. Two-tiered Christian experience is not sustainable from the Bible.

Several years ago, I attended a meeting held for clergy and paid Christian workers. A senior clergyman

---

6   John 1:33
7   John 13:6-10

gave his testimony. He said that he had stopped reading his Bible, and also saying his prayers. He told us that he had stopped preparing sermons and really didn't like church at all. Then God did a wonderful work in his life of restoration. He told us that he had been 'baptized by the Holy Spirit', and that he had been wonderfully restored. He was now reading the Bible, praying, preparing properly and loving his people again. So wonderful was this to him that he urged all of us to seek this baptism by the Holy Spirit for ourselves.

As I listened to this clergyman's experience, I was greatly moved at God's kindness to him. He was a good and godly man. He had been wonderfully dealt with by God. And he knew that if he wanted me to desire this experience he would have to describe it biblically, and he did this by labelling it as the 'baptism by the Holy Spirit'.

However, in this he was mistaken. Whatever his experience was, it was not 'baptism by the Holy Spirit', which in the New Testament is something like being 'born again'.[8] It is the experience of all Christians. However, that does not mean his experience was not real. It had happened. And in God's kindness, it might happen to me as well, or it might not. It does not have to be discounted, but it was not the baptism by the Spirit. That is something different altogether.

---

8   See, for example, 1 Corinthians 12:12-13.

It is also worth pointing out that just because someone has an experience, it doesn't mean that everyone should have it. Paul had an incredible experience where he was taken up into the seventh heaven and saw unutterable sights.[9] That has never happened to me, and nor (I would guess) to many of you. Paul doesn't suggest that we should seek it for ourselves. In fact, he tells us that to stop him becoming too elated he was given a thorn in the flesh, a minister of Satan. Personally, I think I would rather not have the experience and do without the minister of Satan! This experience was personal and not for all.

Another example of this is recorded in Revelation. John, after the seventh trumpet is sounded and the seven thunders sound, is about to write down the message he heard when an angel tells him not to do so, because that message is private. It is for him and his encouragement.[10]

Not all experiences are for all. God deals with us personally and individually for our own good. That which is available for all is told to us in the Bible. I sometimes wonder about our fascination with people's experiences. I think we should perhaps take greater care when we are giving our testimonies. Our experiences are real, but we can be easily mistaken about their meanings.

---

[9] 2 Corinthians 12:1-10
[10] Revelation 10:1-4

Healing ministries

It is a great comfort to know that God cares about every event in our lives, and he encourages us to pray about them. Again and again, the Lord Jesus is described as a man of compassion, especially when he confronts sickness.

It seems impossible to me that if a person is sick, they wouldn't pray about their healing and ask their friends to do so as well. Every church I have ever belonged to has regularly prayed for members who were sick, that they would be healed. In some of the churches I have attended, there have been slots in the Sunday gathering where people were asked to come forward for special prayers for healing.

Some of my friends have experienced marvellous healings as a result of prayer. I haven't. Perhaps I have been shielded by God from disease, but if that is the case only the Day of Judgement will reveal it. Of my chronic diseases I have had to say, with Paul, "Your grace is sufficient for me".[11]

Having said this, you can imagine my surprise when, one Sunday afternoon at the chapel I attend, the preacher posed the question, "Does God want us to be sick?" I should hasten to tell you that I live in a retirement village where the average age of those attending our chapel is about 80. I quickly estimated that collec-

---

[11] 2 Corinthians 12:9

tively we had taken about 500 pills to get us out of bed that morning, another 100 at lunchtime, and we would need another 500 to get us ready for bed. We were all walking medical miracles.

It was an intriguing sermon. We were told that sickness was a result of the fall (with which I totally agreed), and that the death and resurrection of the Lord Jesus had dealt with the results of the fall (with which I partially agreed), and that if we trusted Jesus he would always either heal us or keep us well in this life (with which I agreed not at all). The preacher needed to understand Romans 8:22-23, where we are told that "the whole creation has been groaning ... and not only the creation, but we ourselves ... groan inwardly as we wait eagerly for ... the redemption of our bodies". You see, redemption has been totally paid for in the death and resurrection of the Lord Jesus, but not yet totally applied. I am completely forgiven and my future is assured. Yet because my body has not yet been redeemed, I will grow old. Someday, some part of me will wear out or succumb to a disease, and I will die. Physical death comes to us all, and this is a result of the sinful, fallen world in which we live.

What the preacher in my chapel did was promise us the new creation now.

Does that matter very much? Well, yes it does, because firstly it's a promise that no preacher can deliver on in our fallen, groaning creation. People will still get sick, and everyone will still die. If people are promised healing, and get ongoing sickness instead, what does it do to their faith?

Many years ago I attended a congregation in which one of the young women was diagnosed with leukaemia. Since she had three little boys not yet at school, this was a great challenge to us as a congregation. As a result of our prayers, there was remission of the symptoms for eighteen months. It returned again and did not improve. I visited this lady and her husband just a few days before her death. I told her that I was praying for a miracle. She said that both she and her husband were also. She asked me if I could think of any unqualified promise in God's word that God would heal her.

I answered, "No".

She said, "You would think for the sake of my husband and the boys it would be better for me to be healed, but if I am not then you can be sure that it is not the best thing for them".

Here was a woman with complete trust in God's goodness. Can you think of anything more damaging to say to her than to suggest that if she **really** was trusting God, she would be healed? She couldn't trust God any more than she was. It was as if she had said, "I am totally in God's hands. He can do with me whatever he wills." That sounds like trust to me!

Promising people that it is always God's will for them to be healed is deeply unsettling for the Christian living in this suffering, groaning world. It makes us believe that our faith or our prayers are defective (or both).

This sort of teaching not only creates doubts and discouragement; it also robs us of our hope. If we can have all the blessing of the new creation now—such as complete health—then what do we have to look forward to? Such teaching will never cause us to yearn for and rejoice in the coming glory. It takes our eyes off the glories to come and focuses them on now.

Please don't misunderstand me. The preacher in our chapel was not a wicked man. He was earnest and longing for God to bless us. I'm on his side. But he was misinformed. He needed to study his Bible more and be guided by it. He was unbalanced in his use of the Bible, expounding one part of it so that it was at odds with another.

Prosperity

The 'prosperity gospel' is another form of realized eschatology. It promises that God will bless Christians with riches, success and prosperity now, if only we trust him and his promise.

I remember being asked by a man on the campus of a university in Johannesburg, "Does God want me to be wealthy?"

"Could God trust you with wealth?" was my reply. "Could he trust that you would give it to the poor and use it for the spread of the gospel?"

He smiled and answered, "I don't think so. Not really."

We both smiled. "I think God will give both you and me just enough to get by with!"

I won't deal with the profound flaws in the 'prosperity gospel' here,[12] except to point out the characteristics it shares with the 'sanctification gospel' and the 'healing gospel'. All three begin with the struggles and tensions that Christians experience in the world now—whether in regard to their personal godliness, their physical health or their material circumstances. They then declare that these struggles are entirely unnecessary. They can be resolved now simply by trusting in God. If we only have faith in God, he will give us victory over sin now, victory over all disease now, and victory in our personal wealth and prosperity now.

You can't blame them for wanting the struggle to end. And the things that they long for and promise will one day be ours—in the new creation. In the age to come, we will be joint heirs with Christ. Every blessing will be ours then, but not necessarily now.

---

[12] For a valuable treatment see Brian Rosner, *Beyond Greed*, Matthias Media, Sydney, 2004.

Three words of warning

To conclude this chapter, I'd like to issue three brief words of warning.

The first is not to over-react. As I look back on my own history with this sort of teaching, I can see that I was tempted to react against the errors by going too far in the other direction—and believing that God would never do anything out of the ordinary. This was as unhelpful for me as the teaching I was reacting against. We need to remember that God can do far more abundantly than all that we ask or think, according to his power at work within us.[13] Our prayers should reflect this.

The second point to remember is that Christians don't always grow in precisely the same way or at the same rate. Have you noticed that some Christians seem to make steady progress in their quest for Christlikeness? Day in and day out they press on. Others seem to make progress through some crisis experience where they are 'lifted' into a greater depth of Christlike character. Neither is better than the other. God knows what we are like, and what is best for each of us. What is important is to look to Jesus, and neither to envy each other nor to look down our noses at each other.

Finally, we must be wary of the temptation to relieve the tension of the Christian life in another

---

[13] Ephesians 3:20-21

way—by slipping back into worldliness and simply giving in to the desires of the flesh. It is easy for Christians to become weary in the struggle. If that is you, I beg you to repent. There is no future in this. And the longer you continue down this road, the weaker your view of sin will become. You will find not only that it troubles you less and less, but also that you have forgotten how good and sweet the forgiveness of Christ is.

I think you will find the letter to the Hebrews a great help. The people to whom this was written were tempted to slip back to their old way of life and give up on Christ. The writer reminds them of how wonderful and superior Jesus is to any alternative, and urges them to pay close attention lest they drift away. The church at Laodicea had also become like this, and the Lord Jesus' judgement on them was very severe: "I know your works: you are neither hot nor cold ... So, because you are lukewarm, and neither hot nor cold, I will spit you out of my mouth".[14] If you find that this is where you are at present, please repent while you still have time.

---

[14] Revelation 3:15-16

Chapter 6

LIVING POSITIVELY WITH THE TENSION

So far, I have been talking about the tension that comes from having a foot in two worlds. Before we were Christians, we didn't experience this tension at all. Our condition before we were in Christ is well described in Ephesians 2. Let's look at it again:

> And you were dead in the trespasses and sins in which you once walked, following the course of this world, following the prince of the power of the air, the spirit that is now at work in the sons of disobedience—among whom we all once lived in the passions of our flesh, carrying out the desires of the body and the mind, and were by nature children of wrath, like the rest of mankind. But God, being

rich in mercy, because of the great love with which
he loved us, even when we were dead in our
trespasses, made us alive together with Christ—by
grace you have been saved—and raised us up with
him and seated us with him in the heavenly places
in Christ Jesus, so that in the coming ages he might
show the immeasurable riches of his grace in
kindness toward us in Christ Jesus. (Eph 2:1-7)

We had the illusion of being free because we did whatever we liked. This changed dramatically when we came to Christ. His Spirit set us free from our bondage to sin and death to serve the Lord Jesus Christ as our Saviour and Master. However, the new life we have in Christ brings us into the tension and conflict that is the subject of this book.

I was discussing this with a friend of mine, and he drew my attention to what appeared to be an inconsistency in my argument. He said, "How can Peter say to his readers that they 'rejoice with joy that is inexpressible and filled with glory'[1] if they were experiencing the tension you're talking about? That doesn't sound like tension. It sounds glorious!"

This is a good question. What is joy? And how does it relate to having a foot in two worlds?

Joy is a sense of gladness and wellbeing because of

---

[1]   1 Peter 1:8

something God has done or has promised to do in the future.

In James 1:2 the writer calls on us to count it all joy when various trials come our way. This is because as we wrestle through them we grow stronger in the Christian life. Contemplating the end result gives us joy in the midst of trials. It is not to be confused with happiness, which may or may not accompany joy. It is hard to be happy during times of temptation or testing, but if we contemplate their outcome—a stronger faith in Jesus—it brings joy. It is the knowledge that God has allowed it to happen to us for our growth which is the source of joy.

The writer of the letter to the Hebrews makes a similar comment in chapter 10:

> But recall the former days when, after you were enlightened, you endured a hard struggle with sufferings, sometimes being publicly exposed to reproach and affliction, and sometimes being partners with those so treated. For you had compassion on those in prison, and you joyfully accepted the plundering of your property, since you knew that you yourselves had a better possession and an abiding one. (Heb 10:32-34)

These people had been persecuted. Their property had been confiscated. Yet still they rejoiced because they knew that in the new creation they would have all these things in abundance. Contemplating this brought them joy.

Joy is not a state of continuous euphoria. It is the experience of knowing that God has our best interests at heart in the present, and a glorious inheritance for us in the future. To lose sight of this can rob us of our joy and, like the people who were the recipients of the letter to the Hebrews, we may be tempted to give up in the struggle.

This brings us back to 1 Peter 1, and the verse raised by my friend. The apostle Peter is not describing a perpetually happy group of Christians without problems or struggles. He urges them to remember what God has done and will do for them—how he gave them new birth (verse 3), and an inheritance that cannot perish (verse 4); and how he will shield them and keep them safe by his power to the end (verse 5). Contemplating these blessings will bring them joy, even "though now for a little while, if necessary, you have been grieved by various trials" (verse 6). Peter's readers were able to rejoice because they knew what God had already done for them, and the goal to which they were travelling, namely their salvation (verse 8-9). Peter's readers were not living in some sort of a cloud cuckoo land, where everything was rosy. But they greatly rejoiced, in spite of their circumstances, because they knew that their future was in God's keeping and was absolutely secure.

Do you remember the time Jesus sent out the 72 to preach in all the places where Jesus himself was to visit? Luke records it like this:

> The seventy-two returned with joy, saying, "Lord, even the demons are subject to us in your name!" (Luke 10:17)

However, Jesus said to them:

> "Do not rejoice in this, that the spirits are subject to you, but rejoice that your names are written in heaven." (Luke 10:20)

Real joy is over our ultimate salvation.

Some people have suggested that joy is the deep satisfaction that comes from being of service to other people. If this is the case, it would fit well with the saying recorded about our Lord in Hebrews 12:

> ... looking to Jesus, the founder and perfecter of our faith, who for the joy that was set before him endured the cross, despising the shame, and is seated at the right hand of the throne of God.
>
> Consider him who endured from sinners such hostility against himself, so that you may not grow weary or fainthearted. (Heb 12:2-3)

Whether this is the case or not, I am sure the joy referred to earlier in 1 Peter 1:8 is the wellbeing we experience when we contemplate God's final destiny for us: the salvation of our souls.

There will be tension and struggle in the Christian life because we have a foot in two worlds simultaneously—this world and the next. This is normal and to be expected. But in the midst of the tension there is joy, because we know that the outcome of the tension and struggle is our growth in faith, and ultimately the glorious inheritance God has stored up for us in Christ.

Keep pressing on

The Christian people to whom the Hebrews letter was written were strongly tempted to drift away from Christ. As we have seen, they were under heavy persecution. Their property had been confiscated. Some had been killed. They were beginning to feel that living the Christian life was just too hard. However, again and again the writer urges them not to give up, but to persevere.[2]

Whatever happens, don't give up in the fight against the world, the flesh and the devil. Keep working at the renewed mind. Ask God to give you his Spirit so that when you study the Bible you will understand it and be led by it. Ask him to help you think God's thoughts after him and not to make worldly decisions. Ask for his help so that the world will not squeeze you into its own mould. Keep reminding yourself that the flesh has been crucified, once and for all, with Christ. Consciously put on the armour of God so that you will stand victoriously against the devil and his cunning ways.

---

[2]   Hebrews 2:1-4, 3:12-19, 5:11-14, 10:19-25, 12:14-29

We began the Christian life with repentance and faith, and this is how we continue it, day by day.

Chapter 7

KEEP YOUR EYES ON THE GOAL

As I FINISH, I WANT TO draw your attention to two passages in Romans 8 that have always helped me. Here is the first:

> For we know that the whole creation has been groaning together in the pains of childbirth until now. And not only the creation, but we ourselves, who have the firstfruits of the Spirit, groan inwardly as we wait eagerly for adoption as sons, the redemption of our bodies. For in this hope we were saved. Now hope that is seen is not hope. For who hopes for what he sees? But if we hope for what we do not see, we wait for it with patience. (Rom 8:22-25)

Did you notice in these verses that we are **groaning** as we wait for the redemption of our bodies? This is the norm. This 'groaning' is a term used to describe a woman with labour pains. When a woman goes into labour you know that the birth of the baby is close at hand. There is no time to delay. She is to be taken to hospital straight away. We are in the labour pains of the birth of the new age. We shouldn't think of it as a long way off. It is close at hand. This is no time to give up. Press on. It won't be long now!

And here is the second passage:

> And we know that for those who love God all things work together for good, for those who are called according to his purpose. For those whom he foreknew he also predestined to be conformed to the image of his Son, in order that he might be the firstborn among many brothers. And those whom he predestined he also called, and those whom he called he also justified, and those whom he justified he also glorified. (Rom 8:28-30)

This passage is full of comfort as we wait for the Lord Jesus to return. Notice that God has promised that all things work for our good. Not some—not even most—but **all** things. That is a great promise. The 'good' that God has promised is Christlikeness of character, as the next sentence makes clear. His purpose is for us to be "conformed to the image of his son". God **can** do it because he is sovereign Lord over everything in his creation. God **will** do it because of his promise, and nothing will prevent him from completing this course of action.

Since God has made such a promise, we should make this a matter of prayer and trust. Ask God to continue to make you more and more like the Lord Jesus Christ.

When I was at teacher's college I stayed at home most evenings to study. My father regularly reminded me each year, that this year was the most important year of my life. Social life was non-existent. Why would anyone do that? The answer is easy. I wanted to pass the exams at the end of the year and gain my degree.

I have a friend who competes in triathlons. He competes in Iron Man events. His weekly training program looks like this: Monday morning he swims for 1 hour. In the evening he runs for 45 minutes. On Tuesday he bike rides for 2 hours in the morning and at night he stretches for 30 minutes to increase his core strength. On Wednesday morning he runs up hills for 1 hour and swims for 45 minutes in the evening. Thursday morning he rests (he deserves it!). He swims for 45 minutes in the evening. Friday morning sees him on the bike for 90 minutes and he runs for 2½ hours in the evening. Does he rest on Saturday? Not a bit! To round off the week he's on his bike for a 4-6 hour ride. Does he enjoy this sort of program? He knows that you can't win the prize if you don't train.

When the Olympics were in Sydney, a friend of mine was told by his children that they wanted to be Olympic athletes. I think they were impressed when they saw people on the winner's dais. That was where they wanted to be.

"Right", said their father. "We will all go to Little Athletics next Saturday and start right away."

Off they went! But it wasn't quite the fun they thought it would be. They were sent to run around the oval. It was hard work. After about two months of this they said, "We've changed our minds. We don't want to be Olympic athletes any more", to which the wise father replied, "We have paid the money, so we will keep going until the end of this term".

Physical training is hard work, and takes perseverance. But if you keep training, the results will come.

In his letter to Timothy, Paul says that training for godliness is similar:

> Have nothing to do with irreverent, silly myths. Rather train yourself for godliness; for while bodily training is of some value, godliness is of value in every way, as it holds promise for the present life and also for the life to come. The saying is trustworthy and deserving of full acceptance. For to this end we toil and strive, because we have our hope set on the living God, who is the Saviour of all people, especially of those who believe. (1 Tim 4:7-10)

Notice that Paul is not thinking he can work his way to heaven by trying hard. He has his "hope set on the living God", who is the Saviour of those who believe. All the same, he urges Timothy to keep up the training program of godliness.

God really does know what he is on about. The Bible writers are very strong about the fact that the best is yet to come. They were looking forward to their reward.[1] We will be rewarded beyond our wildest dreams.[2]

Here is a prayer you may like to pray:

Thank you, heavenly Father, for adopting me into your family. Please strengthen me by your Spirit so that I will persevere and not give up. Help me to walk in the Spirit and to put on the whole armour of God. Fill me with your love so that I will want to speak to people about you. Amen.

[1]   2 Timothy 4:6-8
[2]   Luke 19:16-19

Appendix

DISCUSSION GUIDE

THE QUESTIONS THAT FOLLOW are designed to help you discuss the content of *A Foot in Two Worlds* with others—your spouse, your friends or the small group you meet with at church. Use these questions as a way of discussing the content of each chapter and encouraging each other to put God's word into practice.

Chapters 1 and 2: Christianity is not for wimps/This present world

1. What do you think are the best things about being a Christian?

2. What do you think are the hardest things about being a Christian?

3. What does Genesis 1-3 tell us about our present world (and our lives):
   - about how good it is?
   - about why it is so messed up?
4. What are the consequences of the fall?
5. What was Satan's role in the fall of humanity into sin?
6. Read John 8:44, Hebrews 2:14-15 and Ephesians 2:1-3. What do these passages tell us about:
   - the devil and his work?
   - the world we live in?
   - the human heart?

Pray that God will protect you from the devil's lies. Thank God that Jesus has overcome the devil.

Chapter 3: The world to come

1. When you think about the world to come, what do you imagine it will be like?
2. Read Isaiah 11:3-9 and Revelation 21:1-5. What sort of place will the new creation be? How will it differ from this present age?
3. Read 1 John 3:1-3, Colossians 3:1-4 and Revelation 7:9-15. What sort of people will be in the world to come?
4. These wonderful pictures of our future in Christ should captivate and encourage our hearts. But we often neglect to think about them or focus on them. What do you think distracts or diverts us from keeping our eyes on the age to come?

Thank God for the future that awaits people who trust in Jesus. Ask him to help you fix your sights on that future.

Chapter 4: A foot in two worlds

1. In what sense do Christians already belong to the age to come?

2. Read 1 John 2:15-17. How are you most in danger of loving the world or "the things in the world"? What worldly attitudes do you detect in your heart?

3. Re-read the section on page 48 about the 'forest of sin'. Is this how you tend to think about the sin that still dwells within you? Which parts of the 'forest' do you need to attack most urgently?

4. Read Hebrews 12:1-4 and Philippians 3:10-15. In the race that is the Christian life:
   - What is the prize or finish line?
   - What slows us down and hinders us as we run?
   - What should we do as we run?

Ask God to help you 'run the race' until the end. Pray that he would help you long for the next world rather than the things of this world.

Chapter 5: Relieving the tension

1. Summarize what is meant by 'entire sanctification'. Then discuss:
   - What is right and desirable about the idea?
   - What is dangerous or unhelpful about the idea?

2. In this chapter, John Chapman writes: "Not all experiences are for all. God deals with us personally and individually for our own good. That which is available for all is told to us in the Bible. I sometimes wonder about our fascination with people's experiences. I think we should perhaps take greater care when we are giving our testimonies. Our experiences are real, but we can be

easily mistaken about their meanings." Talk about some spiritual experiences you have had, or have heard about from others. What would be the best way to understand those experiences from the Bible?

3. The teachings that God wants us to have perfect health now and prosperity now have been described as 'godly heresies'. Why are they godly? And why are they also mistaken?

4. Re-read the 'Three words of warning' at the close of the chapter. Do any of these particularly challenge you? Why?

Ask God to keep you firm in faith, and for help understanding his promises for this world and the next.

Chapters 6 and 7: Living positively with the tension/ Keep your eyes on the goal

1. What do you think is the difference (if any) between 'joy' and 'happiness'?

2. Read 1 Peter 1:3-9:
   - How would you summarize the experience of the people Peter is writing to?
   - How is this like/unlike your own experience as a Christian?

3. Read Romans 8:22-25. How does this passage describe our present experience in the world?

4. Read Romans 8:28-30. What comfort and reassurance does this passage give us?

5. Try to summarize in a few sentences what it means to live as a Christian with 'a foot in two worlds'.

Thank God that he works in all situations for the good of those who love him. Ask him to help you live faithfully in this world with your eyes fixed on the world to come.

matthiasmedia

Matthias Media is a ministry team of like-minded, evangelical Christians working together to achieve a particular goal, as summarized in our mission statement:

> To serve our Lord Jesus Christ, and the growth of his gospel in the world, by producing and delivering high quality, Bible-based resources.

It was in 1988 that we first started pursuing this mission together, and in God's kindness we now have more than 250 different ministry resources being distributed all over the world. These resources range from Bible studies and books, through to training courses and audio sermons.

To find out more about our large range of very useful products, and to access samples and free downloads, visit our website:

www.matthiasmedia.com.au

How to buy our resources

1   Direct from us over the internet:
    – in the US: www.matthiasmedia.com
    – in Australia and the rest of the world: www.matthiasmedia.com.au

2   Direct from us by phone:
    – in the US: 1 866 407 4530
    – in Australia: 1800 814 360 (Sydney: 9663 1478)
    – international: +61-2-9663-1478

3   Through a range of outlets in various parts of the world. Visit **www.matthiasmedia.com.au/international.php** for details about recommended retailers in your part of the world, including www.thegoodbook.co.uk in the United Kingdom.

4   Trade enquiries can be addressed to:
    – in the US: sales@matthiasmedia.com
    – in the UK: sales@ivpbooks.com
    – in Australia and the rest of the world: sales@matthiasmedia.com.au

Also by John Chapman

A Sinner's Guide to Holiness

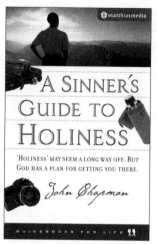

What is holiness? Why do I need it? And why is it such a struggle for me to achieve holiness in my everyday life?

In *A Sinner's Guide to Holiness*, John Chapman explores what the Bible has to say about holiness—where it begins, how it makes progress in our lives, and its ultimate fulfilment as we are changed into Christ's glorious likeness on the Last Day.

This book is a timely publication in this day and age, when we have often lost sight of the holiness of God. And when we do, it seems like an impossible task to achieve our own holiness. But 'Chappo' tells us that becoming holy is a vital, worthwhile goal for every Christian—even though the first 60 years may be the hardest!

A Fresh Start

Something is terribly wrong—with our world, with our relationships, with us. We all sense this at different times. But is there anything that can be done about it?

With all the honesty and humour for which he is famous, John Chapman tells us in *A Fresh Start* that God has done something about it.

We read about:

- just what God has done for us through his Son, Jesus
- how we can know it is true
- what the alternatives are
- what we should do about it.

If you have been searching for a book that simply and clearly explains what it means to be a Christian, either for your own or another's benefit, your search is over.

FOR MORE INFORMATION OR TO ORDER CONTACT:

Matthias Media
Telephone: +61-2-9663-1478
Facsimile: +61-2-9663-3265
Email: info@matthiasmedia.com.au
Internet: www.matthiasmedia.com.au

Matthias Media (USA)
Telephone: 1-866-407-4530
Facsimile: 724-964-8166
Email: sales@matthiasmedia.com
Internet: www.matthiasmedia.com

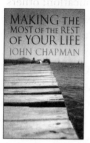

Guidebooks for Life

Bible-based essentials for your Christian journey

Some Christian books are all theory and no practical application; others are all stories and tips with no substance. The Guidebooks for Life series aims to achieve a vital balance—that is, to dig into the Bible and discover what God is telling us there, as well as applying that truth to our daily Christian lives.

We want this series of books to grow into a basic library for every Christian, covering all the important topics and issues of the Christian life in an accessible, straightforward way. Currently the series includes books on holiness, encouragement, prayer, guidance, defending the gospel, and faith.

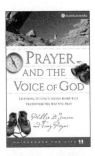

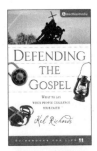

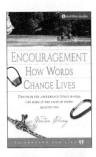

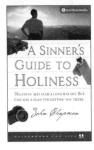

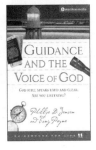

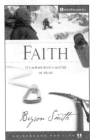

FOR MORE INFORMATION OR TO ORDER CONTACT:

Matthias Media
Telephone: +61-2-9663-1478
Facsimile: +61-2-9663-3265
Email: info@matthiasmedia.com.au
Internet: www.matthiasmedia.com.au

Matthias Media (USA)
Telephone: 1-866-407-4530
Facsimile: 724-964-8166
Email: sales@matthiasmedia.com
Internet: www.matthiasmedia.com